W9-BWL-562

Clothespin Crafts

By Margaret Holtschlag and Carol Trojanowski

Illustrated by Stephanie Roth

A Random House PICTUREBACK® Book

To Margaret and Joe Prendergast
—M. H.

To Joan, who has long appreciated my creative talents
—C. T.

To Josh
—S. R.

Text copyright © 1999 by Margaret Holtschlag and Carol Trojanowski. Illustrations copyright © 1999 by Stephanie Roth. All rights reserved under International and Pan-American Copyright Conventions. Published in the United States by Random House, Inc., New York, and simultaneously in Canada by Random House of Canada Limited, Toronto.
www.randomhouse.com/kids

Library of Congress Cataloging-in-Publication Data

Holtschlag, Margaret. Clothespin crafts / by Margaret Holtschlag and Carol Trojanowski ; illustrated by Stephanie Roth. p. cm. SUMMARY: Provides instructions for using clothespins to make a variety of crafts, including puppets, animals, and airplanes. ISBN 0-679-88645-1. 1. Handicraft—Juvenile literature. 2. Clothespins—Juvenile literature. [1. Clothespins. 2. Handicraft.] I. Trojanowski, Carol. II. Roth, Stephanie, ill. III. Title. TT160.H54 1999 745.5—dc21 98-17181

Printed in the United States of America 10 9 8 7 6 5 4 3 2 1

PICTUREBACK is a registered trademark of Random House, Inc.

INTRODUCTION

You'll be amazed at what a cinch it is to create things with a bagful of clothespins! These simple-to-make projects are perfect for children aged four and up.

A butterfly beauty and a clothespin airplane are just two of the many crafts you can make. Adult assistance with scissors or glue will be helpful, and a creative-minded friend of any age is always useful!

Types of Clothespins

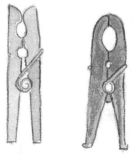

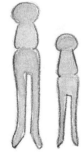

spring-action, wooden and plastic   small and large flat   pinch-style plastic

ClothesPin Organizers

Clothes, toys, and hats are a cinch to put away with this clever organizer!

What You Need

- safety scissors
- string, ribbon, or yarn
- pinch-style plastic clothespins, with holes in the open ends

What You Do

1 Cut a length of string, ribbon, or yarn and tie it to the doorknob or to the clothes bar in your closet.

2 Attach the clothespins to the string at evenly spaced intervals by slipping the string through one of the holes in each clothespin and knotting it.

3 Clip your clothes, hats, or toys on the clothespins.

Refrigerator Hang-Up

These clothespin clips will turn your refrigerator into an art gallery!

What You Need

- safety scissors
- adhesive-backed magnetic strip
- spring-action wooden or plastic clothespins
- markers or non-toxic paint

What You Do

1 Cut a length of magnetic strip to fit the flat side of the clothespin.

2 Peel off the self-stick covering and press the adhesive side of the magnetic strip to the clothespin.

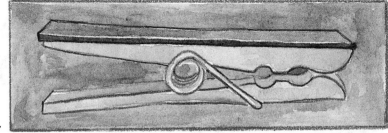

3 Paint and decorate your clothespin. You can even personalize it with your name.

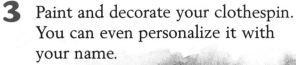

4 Clip pictures, messages, schoolwork, or notes to the clothespin, then place the clothespin, magnet side down, on the refrigerator door.

Clothespin Construction Zone

Build yourself a three-dimensional creation by clipping clothespins together!

What You Need

- spring-action wooden clothespins

- non-toxic paint or markers

What You Do

1 Paint clothespins with bright colors or decorate with markers.

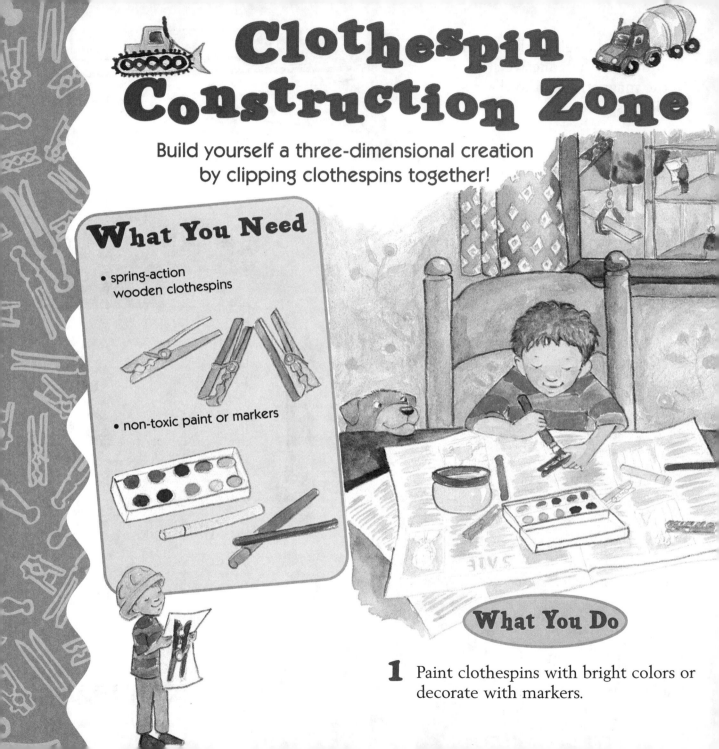

2 Connect the clothespins together to form different shapes.

3 Use your imagination and build monsters—or even a castle!

ClothesPin Coasters

These colorful coasters will be the toast of the town!

What You Need

- small (2½") flat clothespins, 6 per coaster

- non-toxic markers

- felt or cardboard cut in 2½" squares, one per coaster

- craft glue

1 Decorate one side of each clothespin with markers. Be creative and make colorful patterns of dots, stripes, etc.

2 Glue six clothespins together, side by side, alternating top and bottom, to form a square.

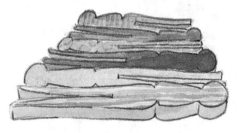

3 Center the clothespins on the felt or cardboard square and glue in place.

4 Set the table and put one coaster at each place setting for a glass or mug.

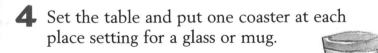

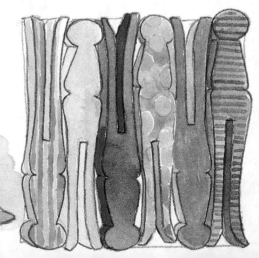

Clothespin Pencil Holder

Tidy up your desk top with this clever container!

What You Need

- approximately 20 flat wooden clothespins

- non-toxic paint or sparkle markers

- empty, clean 6-oz. tuna can

- non-toxic acrylic varnish

What You Do

1 Use paint or sparkle markers to decorate the clothespins.

2 Hook the clothespins onto the rim of the empty can. They should fit snugly side by side.

3 With an adult's help, paint the clothespins with a layer of acrylic varnish and let dry. Be sure to work in a well-ventilated area when using acrylic varnish.

Yackety-Yak Puppet

Let your fingers do the talking with this puppet pal!

What You Need

- safety scissors

- paper plate or stiff paper

- non-toxic markers

- tape

- spring-action wooden or plastic clothespin

What You Do

1 Cut a 3-inch circle from the paper plate.

2 Fold the circle in half, then open it up and lay it flat.

3 Draw an upper lip on the top fold and a lower lip on the bottom fold.

4 With your markers, add eyes, eyebrows, a nose, and hair to the top half and a shirt collar to the bottom half.

5 Cut the circle on the fold, and tape each half to either side of the clothespin.

6 Open and close the clothespin and watch your puppet talk—yackety-yak!

Animal Friends

Make a whole herd of animals out of a bag of clothespins!

What You Need

- small or large flat clothespins

- craft glue

- non-toxic markers

- flat toothpick or yarn

What You Do

1 Glue two flat clothespins together.

2 Next, turn a third clothespin upside down and glue it to one of the clothespins. It should be one third of the way from the top, with its prongs up in the air.

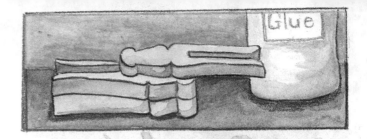

3 Draw eyes, eyebrows, and a nose with your markers.

4 Glue a flat toothpick to the back of the two clothespins for a tail. Or make the tail from a strand of yarn.

5 You can make different animals by adding zebra stripes or giraffe spots, or create an animal of your own design!

Grasshopper Giant

Hop into fun with this oversized insect!

What You Need

- large (3¾")
  flat clothespin
- non-toxic green paint
- paintbrush
- 12" pipe cleaner
- Two 6" pipe cleaners
- non-toxic marker
- 4" pipe cleaner

What You Do

1 Paint the clothespin green and let it dry.

2 Shape a pair of wings from the 12" pipe cleaner, and twist it around the waist of the clothespin.

3 Use the 6" pipe cleaners to fashion two pairs of insect legs, bent at the knees.

4 Slide each pair of legs in place between the prongs of the clothespin, two legs on each side.

5 Use a marker to draw eyes on the head of the grasshopper.

6 To make the antennae, twist the 4" pipe cleaner around the neck of the clothespin, leaving the ends pointing upward.

Playtime Airplane

The sky's the limit with this airborne toy!

What You Need

- safety scissors
- spring-action wooden clothespin
- non-toxic markers or paint
- stick of wrapped gum
- craft glue
- paper
- toothpick
- 3" pipe cleaner
- Two 1" buttons

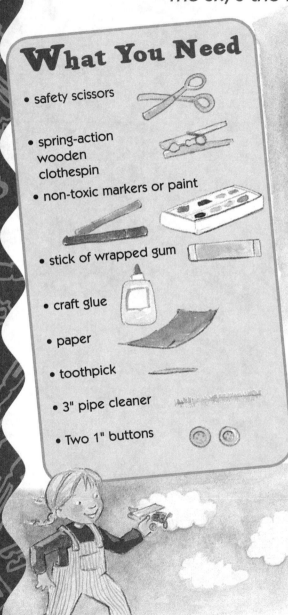

What You Do

1 Decorate a wooden spring-action clothespin with markers or paint. This is the body of your airplane.

2 For wings, glue a stick of gum on the flat side of the clothespin about one-third of the way from the closed end (the nose of the plane).

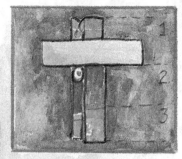

3 Cut a small propeller from a piece of paper.

4 Break a toothpick in half. Stick the toothpick through the middle of the paper propeller.

5 Attach the propeller by pinching the clothespin open and inserting the toothpick into it.

6 To attach airplane wheels, bend the 3-inch piece of pipe cleaner into an upside-down "V" and slip it through the clothespin, near the spring. Then fasten the two 1-inch buttons to the ends of the pipe cleaner for wheels.

Butterfly Beauties

Fly away with these hand-dyed butterflies!

What You Need

- 4 paper cups
- red, yellow, blue, and green food coloring
- paper towel
- large flat clothespin
- 4" pipe cleaner
- non-toxic marker

What You Do

1 Using four cups, mix a few drops of red, yellow, blue, and green food coloring with ¼ cup of cold water in each cup.

2 Fold a paper towel in eighths and dip each of the four corners of the paper towel in a different color. Then carefully unfold and let dry.

3 Fold your paper towel like a fan. First, fold 1 inch of the towel one way, then turn it and fold it over the other way. Continue until the entire paper towel is folded.

4 Slip the center of the fan-folded paper towel between the prongs of the clothespin and gently unfold the towel. These are the wings.

5 Twist the 4-inch piece of pipe cleaner around the neck of the clothespin for antennae.

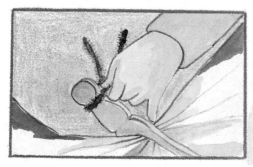

6 With your marker, draw eyes and a mouth on the head of the clothespin.

Bonus Page

This page is a place for you to think up some of your own ideas for using clothespins. Here's one more.

Paper clips, buttons, and coins all in a jumble?
Let's get them in order with this sort-and-store organizer!

1 Decorate small boxes with markers, stickers, or different colors of paint.

2 Add glitter to the clothespins or draw designs with markers.

3 Fasten the sides of the boxes together with clothespins.

4 Sort small objects into the containers, or arrange the boxes for a penny-tossing game!

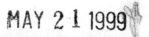